T0162620

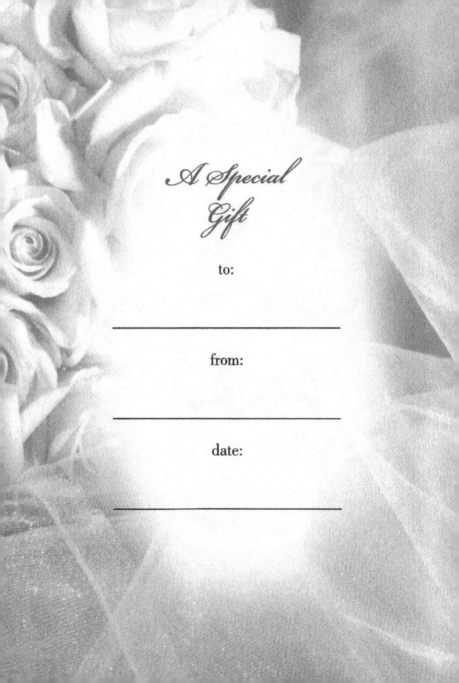

*A Special
Gift*

to:

_____

from:

_____

date:

_____

Stories, sayings, and scriptures to Encourage and Inspire the ...

hugs™

for
those in Love

RON AND LYN ROSE

Personalized Scriptures by
LEANN WEISS

HOWARD
PUBLISHING CO.

Our purpose at Howard Publishing is to:

- *Increase faith* in the hearts of growing Christians
- *Inspire holiness* in the lives of believers
- *Instill hope* in the hearts of struggling people everywhere

Because He's coming again!

Hugs for Those in Love © 2000 by Ron and Lyn Rose
All rights reserved. Printed in the United States of America

Published by Howard Publishing Co., Inc.,
3117 North 7th Street, West Monroe, LA 71291-2227

06 07 08 09 10   15 14 13 12

Personalized scriptures by LeAnn Weiss, owner of Encouragement Company,
3006 Brandywine Dr., Orlando, FL 32806; 407-898-4410.

Interior design by LinDee Loveland

Library of Congress Cataloging-in-Publication Data

Rose, Ron.
   Hugs for those in love : stories, sayings, and scriptures to encourage and inspire
/ Ron and Lyn Rose ; personalized scriptures by LeAnn Weiss.
   p. cm.
ISBN: 978-1-4767-4800-9
   1. Spouses—Religious life. 2. Marriage—Religious aspects—Christianity. I.
Rose, Lyn. II. Weiss, LeAnn. III. Title.

BV4596.M3 R67 2000
248.8'44—dc21

                                    00-027183

Contents

Of all the earthly music, that which reaches farthest into heaven is the beating of a truly loving heart.

—Henry Ward Beecher

Three little words,
"I love you,"
are the words that
topple empires, shape
destinies, make men
and women risk their lives
and unite millions of couples
in holy matrimony
every year.
What power is in those words!

—Nancy Corbett Cole

CHAPTER ONE

Bringing Out the Best

$\mathcal{I}$’ve caused you to leave your parents to join your lives together forever. You’re no longer two, but one. You’re able to love because I first loved you! Don’t just love with words; demonstrate your love with action and in truth. Learn the secret of being content in every situation.

Uniting You,

Your God of Peace

—from Mark 10:7–8; 1 John 4:19; 3:18; Philippians 4:12

Higgins Photography

Love is a gift that takes a lifetime to unwrap. Just when we think we've figured it out, we discover something new that changes everything. As we grow older and more willing to live in the present—without feeling trapped by the past or worried about the future—we realize this gift has many dimensions. There's a sensual side; an affectionate and romantic side; a compassionate and tender side; a fun-loving, surprising side; a strategic, problem-solving side; and a practical side; just to name a few. The gift of love has many components.

All lifelong, intimate relationships are built on the promise to be a giver of this gift. The mystery is that the more love we give, the more we have to give—the supply continues to grow, unendingly. We receive love even when we don't deserve it.

When the doors are closed and the lights are off, we all have our share of undesirable habits and quirky secrets. Lifelong love, grace-love, what the Bible calls *agape* love, is the gift of seeing the best in each other, regardless.

This kind of love is rare, and we must experience it before we can give it.

This gift of love refuses to label or limit others. It inspires and encourages and lifts others, whether we feel like it or not. Instead of controlling and dominating a lover, it finds ways to see the good and bring out the best in spite of the circumstances.

This may sound unrealistic. It is, to those who have not experienced it. To Christians, however, it is a reflection of God's love.

When our relationships are born in the heart of God, they bring out the best in us, for they are nurtured by love.

—Don Lessin

"Dad, what's your secret?
You and Mom have
always been so much in
love. Please tell me."

Mom's Little Secret

The ceremony was arranged, the rehearsal festivities had gone well, and Kate's dad was staying up late, as usual. He sat in his favorite chair on the deck, looking up toward the stars but not seeing any of them. It had been a long day, and the anticipation of Kate's wedding was playing in his mind like a film from long ago. As he was enjoying the moment, the door opened, interrupting his reverie.

It was Kate—an unexpected but pleasant interruption.

"What's up, kid?" he asked.

"Can I sit here for just a bit?" she asked, ignoring his question.

"Of course," Dad responded, making room. "This reminds me of when you were a little girl and you'd come out here when you couldn't sleep. You know, everything will be different after tomorrow, and that's the way it should be. I couldn't be happier for you and David."

For a bit, they reviewed the day, laughing over the hilarious family video they'd watched at the rehearsal dinner. They also shed a tear or two as both realized this would be their last night together as "Dad and his little girl."

Their relationship was about to change in some indescribable, unexperienced way.

After a period of silence, Kate asked, "Dad, what's your secret? You and Mom have always been so much in love. Please tell me."

"Kate," her Dad confessed, "it's not my secret—it's your mom's. From the day we met, she has made it her life's goal to bring out the best in me."

"What do you mean?" Kate asked.

"When we began dating, she introduced me as the last of the grand gentlemen. Your mom made it easy for me to be a grand gentleman to her. I courted her as if she were a queen; all I desired was to win her heart. After we married, she bragged to her friends that I was the best listener in the world, that I really understood her. And she helped me learn to listen, to listen beyond the words, to listen for the sake of listening. It was tough for me. It took a lot of time. I wanted a shortcut, some way to solve the problems and fix whatever was broken. But she just wanted me to listen. It seemed strange, but as she gently taught me, I really learned how to listen."

"Didn't you feel like she was trying to change you all the time?" Kate quizzed. "What happened when you didn't measure up?"

He leaned up in his chair and looked deep into his daughter's eyes. "Kate, your mom loves me, regardless. That's what we promised to each other on our wedding day. She doesn't require me to be better in order to be loved; she loves me in spite of my failures, not just when I am good or because I am good."

"I'm not sure I understand," Kate declared. "Are you talking about grace or love?"

"Both," Dad answered. "They're sort of the same thing. Love makes you a dispenser of grace. Your mom doesn't love me because I love her or when I love her; she loves me because she promised to love me—in spite of my failures, struggles, or stubbornness."

"You know, Dad," Kate affirmed, "you do the same thing for Mom."

"I've tried to," he answered.

Kate reached out, took her dad's hand, and slipped into his lap. She hugged him like she had when she was a child, only this time was even more special. It marked a moment of truth between father and daughter that would outlive them both.

After a bit, Dad said, "You know, all my life I've been a better person because your mother loved me, and now you have the opportunity to help David become a better man too."

"I will always love you, Dad. You and Mom have given me more than you will ever know. David doesn't realize it yet, but he's going to be the best husband ever."

Kate left her dad sitting in his chair on the deck, looking toward the stars but not seeing any of them.

14

Reflections . . .

What secrets have you observed in other marriages or your own that have helped love grow?

_____

_____

_____

_____

_____

_____

_____

_____

_____

_____

_____

_____

_____

_____

CHAPTER TWO

Appreciating

Differences

*L*et love be your motivation. Be completely humble and gentle, practicing patience as you bear with one another in love. When you accept one another just as Christ accepted you, you bring praise to Me. I'll give you a spirit of unity between you as you follow My Son together, cheering each other on to love and good deeds.

Love,

Your God of Encouragement

—from 1 Corinthians 16:14; Ephesians 4:2; Romans 15:5–7;

Hebrews 10:24

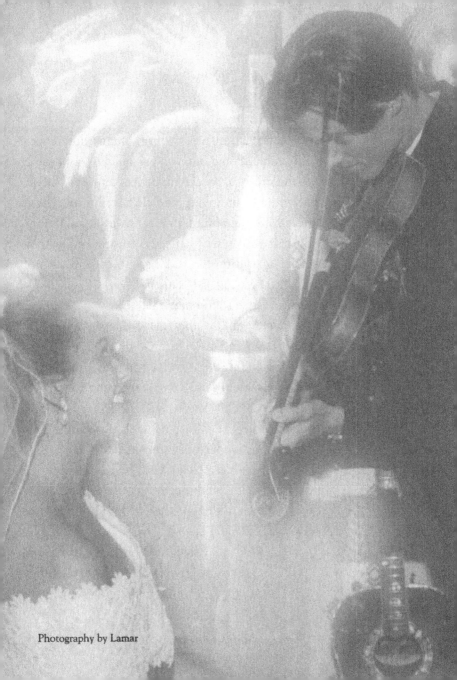

Photography by Lamar

In a relationship, we bring many differences to the table. Some of them are quickly noticeable and wonderfully appreciated; others, however, lie in the background, annoying and distracting us. These differences have the potential to eat away at a relationship, killing it with resentment and frustration, or they can energize a relationship, taking it to new worlds of adventure and new levels of trust.

Do any of these sound familiar?

– He avoids failure and seeks independence; she avoids isolation and seeks intimacy.

– She wants to talk, just to talk; he'll talk when there is a problem to solve or something to fix.

– She quickly stops and asks for directions, even before she's lost; he feels that asking for directions is a sign of weakness.

– She has a clean desk; he has a roll top.

– He's working to recover from a turbulent childhood; she's living in a fairy-tale world.

– She grows spiritually by becoming involved in every church ministry; he grows spiritually by escaping to the mountains for some time alone with God.

– He is a conservative Republican; she hasn't told him, but she didn't even vote in the last election.

– She talks in order to sort out her thoughts; he won't speak until he has thought it all out.

– He thrives on risk; she avoids risk.

Our differences form a path to mutual understanding. We can walk that path and learn to appreciate each other, or we can complain about the conditions and never even begin the journey. Learn to embrace and celebrate your differences.

The combination of our differences makes us unique. After all, no couple in the world has our assortment of differences.

We were created with these differences for a reason—to shape, refine, admonish, enrich, and balance each other. We transform each other as though we become the hands of God. We cannot become our best without our counterparts.

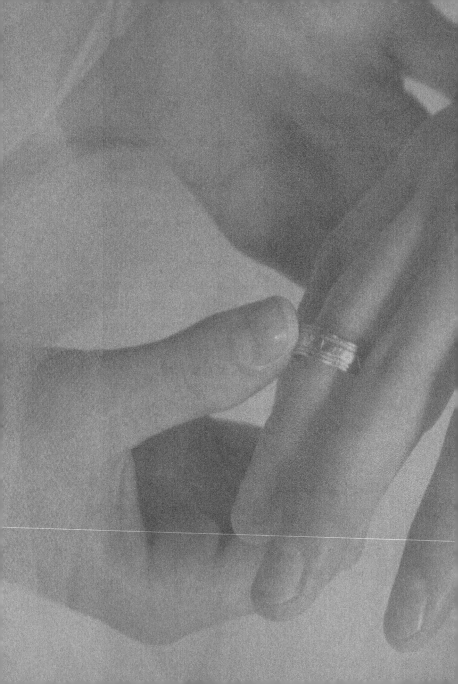

Love is the expansion of two natures in such a fashion that each includes the other, each is enriched by the other.

—Felix Adler

Most of their best talks took place when they traveled late at night.

What a Strange Thing to Say

On an evening nearing his one-month wedding anniversary, Jim was relaxing in his first new piece of furniture, the recliner—the "man" chair. Finally, he felt like a real grownup. However, not everything was complete; the greatest invention of the modern world—the TV remote control—had not yet found its way to Jim's living room.

Carol was in the kitchen fiddling with

something, and Jim called to her to ask for a glass of tea. If he worked it right, she would function as his remote control, and Jim wouldn't have to get up. His plan was to get her to change the channel on her way back to the kitchen.

But Carol evidently had a different idea. Handing the tea to Jim, she preempted his request with, "It's time to take out the garbage, hon."

She caught Jim off guard, and he forgot to ask her to change the channel.

Jim thought, *What a strange thing to say.* Why would she tell him what she was about to do? He didn't make an announcement every time he washed the car or mowed the lawn.

Then, Carol repeated herself, only this time with a louder voice and a touch of frustration.

"Did you hear me? It's time to take out the garbage!"

That's her job, Jim thought to himself. *She's violating the natural order of things. Men do the outside stuff, and women do the inside stuff. My mother took care of the garbage in the house, and my dad dealt with it outside. That's the way it's supposed to be.*

Not only was Carol requesting something unnatural, she was already turning into his mother. She was telling Jim what to do and when to do it. He suddenly saw his future unfold before him: He was going to be hen-pecked the rest of his life.

Why can't she just keep quiet? Jim thought. *I'll take out her garbage in a little bit—when it's my idea.*

But this time she meant business: "Jim, get out of that chair and take care of this garbage!"

Jim took out the garbage, but he didn't like it, and he sulked for a week.

This pattern was repeated over and over again for months, until Jim and Carol returned to their hometown for Christmas vacation. As strange as it felt to spend the night in Carol's old bed with her parents in the next room, something else seemed even more strange. Jim noticed that Carol's dad had evidently missed the outside/inside job-description bulletin. Each night he made the rounds through the house gathering trash, and each night he took all the trash outside. No wonder Carol expected Jim to take care of the garbage. Her dad took out the family trash daily, thus sabotaging Jim's idea of the natural division of labor.

Once the holidays ended, Jim and Carol headed home. It was a long trip, but to save the cost of a motel room, they decided to drive all night. About 3:00 A.M., they were talking about all sorts of stuff, just to keep each other awake. In fact, most of their best talks took place when they traveled late at night. It was dark, and Jim didn't have to look into Carol's eyes, so he could talk about anything.

"I guess you've noticed that I've had an attitude problem about the garbage," Jim opened.

"I know," she responded.

29

"Well, I saw your dad doing the garbage detail, and now I understand why you think I should take it out. I've just never considered the garbage my job. Don't get me wrong; it's no big deal. I just don't want to be told to do it. You're my wife, not my mother," Jim explained.

Then, he added, almost as an afterthought, "I just want it to be my idea, okay?"

"Sure," Carol said, "I can live with that."

For a while neither talked; then the conversation moved on to hunger, and they decided to search for somewhere to stop for a snack.

A couple of days after Jim and Carol returned home, the garbage stacked up pretty high under the sink. With her newfound knowledge of Jim's views on the garbage, Carol stood at the doorway to the kitchen and asked,

"Honey, is it your idea to take out the garbage yet?"

"It sure is," Jim answered. "It's my idea to do the garbage detail at the next commercial."

It worked for them!

Reflections . . .

What "strange things" did you or your spouse bring to your marriage? What have you learned about compromise and give-and-take?

_____

_____

_____

_____

_____

_____

_____

_____

_____

_____

_____

_____

_____

_____

CHAPTER THREE

Activating

Romance

$\mathcal{W}$alk in love. Remember, love is patient and kind. It's not self-seeking or easily angered. Love always protects, always trusts, always hopes, and always perseveres. Be kind and compassionate to each other, forgiving each other's shortcomings just like Christ forgave you.

Compassionately,

Your Heavenly Father

—from 2 John 1:6; 1 Corinthians 13:4–7; Ephesians 4:32

Dozens of roses, alluring environments, candlelight dinners—these do not define romance. It cannot be measured in dollars spent or gifts received. Romance is the unexpected escape from the stresses of life. It's an intimate message that speaks of value and importance. In short, it refocuses and energizes a relationship.

A marriage without romance is dull, dominated by routine and scheduled by boredom. Marriage was designed from the beginning to preserve romance, not eliminate it. We are never too old to rekindle our efforts at romance. Little surprises can make a big difference: Hold hands while you walk. Call each other during the day. Go out for a Coke or a cup of coffee. Send a card or a letter that describes your love. Serve together in a ministry that focuses on helping those less fortunate than you. Watch an old movie together. Organize your pictures together.

It takes a little planning to keep romance alive year after

year. And those plans must translate into action. Good intentions don't count. We have to write the notes and slip them into the glove box. We have to call the hotel and make the reservations. We have to order the flowers, send the cards, take the walks, buy the chocolate, build the fire, draw the bath. Only when we actually do these things do they turn into romance.

Romance is our most effective method for communicating feelings. When we take romantic action, we communicate our love, even if we don't have the words to describe those feelings.

Knowing we are loved is not enough. Saying the words, "I love you," is not enough. We long to feel we are loved. Romance sends that feeling to the heart. It doesn't matter what it costs or what others think, as long as that heart message is sent and received. When we feel loved, we feel valuable, needed, special, extraordinary. Amazing, isn't it? Romance is not an option.

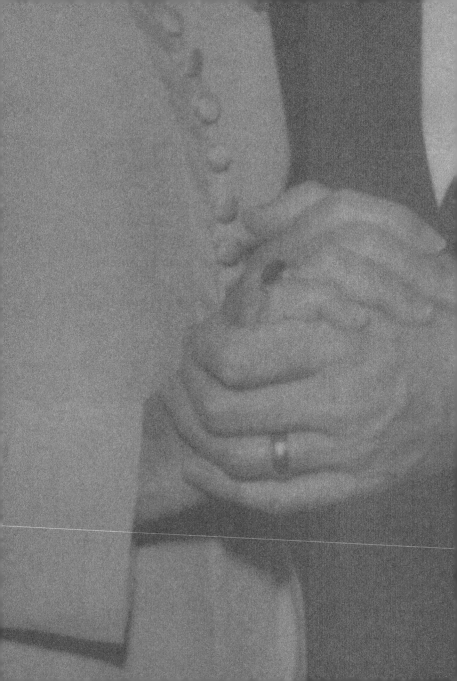

For love is but the heart's immortal thirst to be completely known and all forgiven.

—Henry Van Dyke

He loved to show off his
new car, but so far, he
had given no one else
the opportunity to
drive his dream.

The Note Had Her Name on It

Michael had finally been able to buy his dream car. The kids were grown and on their own. Kristen's car was only two years old and in great shape. He had needed a new car, so why not go for the dream?

The '65 Mustang was in "better-than-new" condition. Granted, it didn't have all the electronics and fancy new gadgets, but it was a classic; Michael felt young and cool driving it around town and back and forth to work. He lived for the weekends when he and Kristen could cruise the countryside.

Of course, he kept his pride and joy sparkling. Whenever he had a spare moment, he spent it in the garage tinkering, polishing, and admiring his dream car. He loved to show it off, but so far, he had given no one else the opportunity to drive his dream.

But one afternoon, Kristen had to do some last-minute shopping for a party they planned to throw that evening. Her car was still in the shop because some out-of-stock computer chip had to be shipped from the West Coast.

When she'd asked Michael to take her to the market for the stuff she needed, his response had nearly stopped her heart. Throwing her his keys, he'd called, "You take my car. I've got to finish the lawn."

"Oh, no!" she'd shrieked. "What if something happens?"

"Honey, it's okay! You'll do fine," he'd returned.

Kristen had reluctantly gotten into the car and carefully driven to the market. After she'd gotten everything on her list, the bagger helped her put her sacks in the trunk.

"Nice car," he volunteered as he closed the trunk.

"It's my husband's," Kristen said as she carefully started the dream car and drove off. She was only two blocks from home when she looked down for just a moment to change the radio station. At that instant a dog ran into

45

the street, and the driver of the pickup in front of her slammed on his brakes to avoid the animal. She stood on the brakes and swerved to the right, but it was too late.

She'll never forget the sound of crunching metal as the front left fender clipped the unyielding truck bumper. No one was hurt, not even the dog. But Kristen was in hysterics.

"Michael! Michael! He'll never forgive me," she cried.

All she could do was sit there and sob. The driver of the pickup truck asked if she was hurt.

"You can't imagine how much I'm hurt," she cried.

"Do you need an ambulance?" he asked.

Finally getting a little control, she shook her

head and responded, "Not now, but I may when my husband sees his car."

The truck driver introduced himself as Mr. Dunn. After looking over the damage, he assured her that she could still drive the car, but he needed to get her insurance information.

Kristen opened the glove box for the insurance papers. The small compartment held only a plastic protective envelope. Inside she found all the necessary insurance and registration papers—and a folded piece of notebook paper with her name on it. She quickly handed the insurance papers to Mr. Dunn.

"Here's what you need," she said.

Then, without another word, she turned her attention to the piece of paper with her name

47

on it. She couldn't open it fast enough. She wondered what it could be. It didn't take long to read. She was speechless, and her tears were unstoppable.

"Are you sure you're all right?" Mr. Dunn asked, concerned by her fresh tears.

Kristen couldn't answer. She handed him the note.

It read: "Kristen, if you are reading this, you've had an accident. Remember, it's you I love, not the car."

In a few days the fender was as good as new. Kristen, on the other hand, was better than new.

48

Reflections . . .

What special memories do you have of a time your spouse "surprised" you with kindness?

_____

_____

_____

_____

_____

_____

_____

_____

_____

_____

_____

_____

_____

CHAPTER FOUR

Marking Milestones

$\mathcal{L}$earn to number your days, that you may gain a heart of wisdom. Think about good times, remember the excellent and praiseworthy moments. Let your love be sincere, as you cling to what is good. Surely goodness and mercy will follow you both all the days of your lives.

Blessing You,

Your God of Every Good and Perfect Gift

—from Psalm 90:12; Philippians 4:8; Romans 12:9; Psalm 23:6

Photography by Lamar

There is always something to learn about love and marriage. Every marriage has anchor points or milestones that define the relationship: people that mean a lot to us and events that change us.

Of course, the wedding itself is an important anchor point, but so is the date when you "knew" this was the one, the time you met the potential in-laws, and the moment of the proposal.

Another milestone is that first conflict that forced you into a more realistic view of each other. Your first trip as a married couple, your first Christmas, your first anniversary, your first move, and your first crisis also mark the way.

Children are anchor points of a marriage at several stages. The period of time from conception to birth is a milestone; and that's just the beginning. Children's first words, steps, school days, class programs, soccer games, weekends with grandparents, and questions about God can and should be anchor points for the marriage.

While children tend to demand our time during their growing-up years, the marriage still needs special times free of their demands. Trips with other couples, marriage projects, and anniversaries are potential anchor points in a strong marriage.

All crisis times are milestones. Health problems, job changes, faith struggles, and grief provide chances for couples to pull together and offer support. Your children's teen years are filled with one crisis after another. During these years, it's easy to take the marriage for granted and end up passing each other in the night. A gentle hug or a walk around the block may end up becoming an important anchor point.

To turn a moment into an anchor point for your marriage, you need to do three things:

1. Experience the moment as a couple.

2. Talk about it. Share your joys, your sadness, your pain, your fears, and your dreams.

3. Take pictures or describe the moment in a journal or do both.

The more anchor points you have, the more aware you become of the value of your marriage and the less likely you will be to cash in such a valuable treasure.

*Love is not
a matter of
counting the
years—it's
making the
years count.*

—Jack Smith Wolfman

As soon as the counselor asked how he could help, Melissa began to cry uncontrollably.

Help from Strange Places

Melissa didn't know where to turn. The counselor on TV seemed to have answers for others. Maybe he could help her. She was a first-time caller, and she wasn't sure what to expect. But she felt desperate, so she dialed the number. After a wait, she finally got her turn to be on the air.

As soon as the counselor asked how he could help, Melissa began to cry uncontrollably.

Between the tears, she managed to explain that she was sure her marriage was falling apart. Her husband, Jared, was beginning to take her for granted, and she was afraid they would have a marriage in form only, without romance or oneness.

The counselor let her unburden herself for a while, then he interrupted and asked how long she and Jared had been married.

"Three weeks," she responded, embarrassed.

"Now, what has Jared done that leads you to believe that your marriage is in trouble?" asked the counselor.

Melissa let it all out. Why not? She was anonymous on the TV call-in show. "Well, as soon as he got home from work tonight, he headed straight for the hall closet and got out his bowling ball. Then he kissed me and announced that he was going bowling with some buddies from work. Why would he want to go bowling with the guys? He should want to be with me. Something's going wrong. He's already taking me for granted. I can see it now. Our marriage is over."

The counselor helped her calm down, and then he suggested that Jared was probably acting in a fairly normal manner. "Just because a couple is married doesn't mean that a spouse can take the place of all relationships. We still need friends and family. I bet he'll come home and want to tell you all about his bowling," he said.

After planting that thought, the counselor gave Melissa a task. In a little over a minute, he'd found out that before Melissa and Jared were married they had gone to a local McDonald's every Thursday evening for a special dinner. The fast-food chain would reserve them a table in the corner, and Melissa and Jared would enjoy a candlelight dinner with a white tablecloth, china plates, and silverware they had brought from home. It was a tradition they had loved. Nearby diners always thought it was especially romantic.

"Melissa," the counselor suggested, "I want you to get out all the pictures you have of when you two were dating. Select the ones that remind you of special events or special people you spent time with before you married. Also, call that McDonald's and reserve your old table for this Thursday evening. Then, take the pictures with you. After you have eaten your Big Macs, look through the pictures together and talk about the events and the people that have enriched your marriage. Can you do that?"

With renewed hope and anticipation, Melissa responded, "Yes, yes I can. Thank you."

Melissa had found just the help she needed. She couldn't wait to hang up the phone and get busy with her plans.

She and Jared didn't have many pictures, but the ones she found reminded her of several wonderful times. The pictures of other people especially drew her attention. She had been so absorbed in her new marriage that she had forgotten how many friends they'd had before they got married. She knew it would be different now, but she made a list of the people she wanted to have lunch with and stay in touch with. Trips, adventures, crazy times, church retreats, family dinners, ball games—she had such fun reliving the memories.

Meanwhile, the TV counseling program continued. Other people were waiting for help and hope.

Then just before the closing moments of the program, Melissa was back on the line with news that she just had to share.

"Melissa, you're back. What's the problem?" asked the counselor.

Melissa was ecstatic. "Nothing!" she fairly screamed. "My husband was watching your show. Can you believe it? He was waiting for his friend to get ready for bowling, and your

64

program was on his friend's TV. Jared called just

a moment ago and told me to gather up the pic-

tures and the china and candles. I can't believe

it! He invited me to McDonald's *tonight!*"

Reflections . . .

What are some of the favorite "anchor points" of your marriage? What makes them so special?

_____

_____

_____

_____

_____

_____

_____

_____

_____

_____

_____

_____

_____

_____

_____

CHAPTER FIVE

Choosing to Be Best Friends

$\mathcal{T}$wo are better than one. When you love one another, I live in you and My perfect love is made complete in you. May love and faithfulness be essential attributes of your lives, forever written on the tablets of your hearts. Remain in My love as you wait for the mercy of Jesus Christ to bring you to eternal life!

Faithfully,

Your God of Love

—from Ecclesiastes 4:10–12; 1 John 4:12; Proverbs 3:3; Jude 21

We have casual friends, people we gather with for activities. Then there are the milestone friends, people from our past with whom we share common stories. Along the way we select a few mentor friends who inspire us and bless us and give us their wisdom. However, we have few best friends.

Best friends know each other's strengths and weaknesses. They know the secrets, and they keep the secrets. And best friends are there during crisis times. Friendship at this level requires lots of time and complete reciprocity. In other words, it's impossible to be best friends with someone who is not best friends with you.

The marriage relationship is designed to transform men and women into best friends. Although their initial attraction may have been hormonal or casual, becoming best friends gives their sexual relationship energy. Without this energy from the growing friendship, sexual intimacy will die.

Marriage has a way of making us choose to be best friends—or not. Building a best-friend relationship takes both time and the willingness to risk. We can choose to let the crisis moments tear off the masks we wear, or we can allow our spouses to help us take the masks off, one layer at a time. The quicker we get past the pretension and fearfulness, the faster we can get on track to becoming best friends before a crisis hits.

When best friends are married to each other for a long time, they can finish each other's sentences. They know each other's thoughts, beliefs, and expectations. As close friends, they share feelings, intentions, goals, motives, needs, successes, and failures. When crisis times hit, we each need a trusted friend who will listen and understand and help us find what we need to deal with the crisis. That trusted friend is the one who knows us better than we know ourselves.

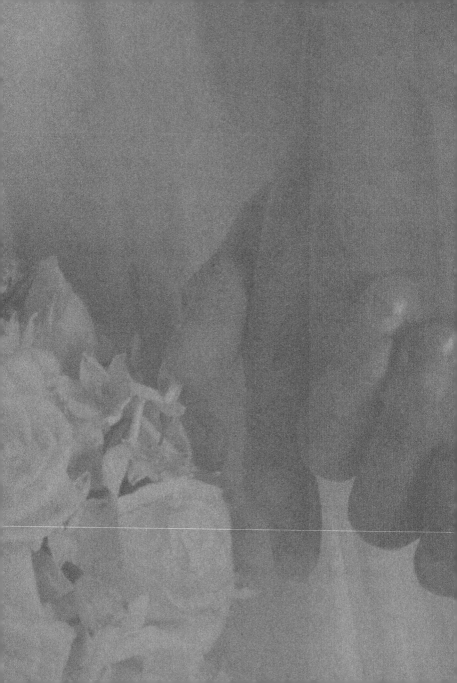

When the truest part of one soul meets the emptiest recesses in another and finds something there...life passes from one to the other.

—Larry Crabb

The gentle, selfless love
they heard in her voice had
been nurtured over a
lifetime, and she proudly
wore her age and her
wrinkles as a badge
of faithfulness.

He's My Best Friend

She had been at his bedside for three days. Tired as she was, no amount of urging could convince her to go home and rest. In fact, her presence was causing scheduling problems. Suddenly, hospital staff wanted to give up days off and work extra shifts just to be around her.

There was something about her gentle spirit and her confident take on life that was infectious and somewhat angelic. She became a frequent subject of conversation at the nurses' station and in the break room. Everyone respectfully called her Mrs. Calabrese. Nurses and doctors alike took turns checking Mr. Calabrese's vitals because they wanted to talk with her.

The gentle, selfless love they heard in her voice had been nurtured over a lifetime, and she proudly wore her age and her wrinkles as a badge of faithfulness. It was clear to everyone who met Mrs. Calabrese that her best friend was the silent man whose hand she gently, constantly held. Stories about her husband flowed from her lips the moment someone entered the room. He was her lifelong investment, and they had been best friends from the beginning. Nothing had been too difficult for them to handle together. It would take years to uncover all the secrets they shared.

Once she asked a doctor who was checking her husband's chart, "Don't you think we look alike? I think so; it happens, you know."

What a rare treat it was to share a few moments of her life.

Mr. Calabrese hadn't moved in days. His life was ebbing away as he slipped in and out of a coma. The doctors tried to prepare Mrs. Calabrese for her husband's imminent death, but she refused to listen. Her life had been intertwined with his for decades. She had helped him through scores of impossible situations, and she would help him through this one too.

Her hands were mysterious. They were time-worn and misshapen, but her slightest touch brought comfort and peace. As she sat in his room, she would not let go of Mr. Calabrese's hand. It was as though their hands belonged together. She might very well be able to baffle the medical experts and bring Mr. Calabrese home one more time.

In the middle of the night, while she slept, Mr. Calabrese suddenly awoke from his coma. Holding his hand was the bride of his youth— his best friend, the woman who had promised to love him till death. The thought of leaving her was unbearable. Knowing death was at the door, he quietly and tenderly relished the touch of her hand for as long as he had breath. His hands had always been empty without her loving clasp. Her hands were nicked and bruised from a lifetime of working with him. Together as friends, they had traveled the uneasy road of life. So many times she had rescued him, lifted him, comforted him, and caressed him.

He couldn't bring himself to awaken her just so she could watch him die, so he wrote her a note. And he lived just long enough to finish his expression of love for his forever-faithful friend.

With only the soft glow of a bedside lamp to guide him, Mr. Calabrese used his free hand to drag a pad and pen from the table to his bed. Then, with tears running down his cheeks, he penned his message, which later became the beautiful words to the familiar song of the '50s.

> Softly, I will leave you softly,
>
> For my heart would break if you
>
> should wake and see me go.

> So I leave you softly, long before you
>
> miss me,
>
> Long before your arms can beg me stay
>
> For one more hour or one more day.
>
> After all the years, I can't bear the
>
> tears to fall.
>
> So, I leave you softly. . . .

When the beep of the heart monitor signaled her husband's death, Mrs. Calabrese awoke. She was still holding her best friend's hand, though he had gone to his eternal home to await her. She noticed the verse her husband had left her, and as she read it, she thought to herself, *That's just like him. He was my best friend for life.*

Reflections . . .

In what ways do you and your spouse share a "friend" relationship? How has that special dimension of love enhanced your marriage?

_____

_____

_____

_____

_____

_____

_____

_____

_____

_____

_____

_____

_____

_____

CHAPTER SIX

Investing

in Others

Photography by Lamar

$\mathcal{E}$ncourage and build each other up. Live a life of love, following the example of My Son who loved you and gave Himself for you as a fragrant offering and sacrifice. I'll make your love increase and overflow for each other and for everyone else, making you rich in every way so that you can be generous on every occasion.

Gloriously,

Your God of Fulfillment

—from 1 Thessalonians 5:11; Ephesians 5:2;
1 Thessalonians 3:12; 2 Corinthians 9:11

One of the oft-forgotten keys to deeper intimacy is working as a team for the benefit of others.

The purpose of life is not just to build a strong marriage, but to share life with others. Nothing strengthens intimacy and oneness like getting your focus off your marriage and onto a mission.

Some couples seem to hold back, waiting for crisis moments to thrust them into some outside mission. Others allow the constant demands of parenting children to detract them from serving others. But as couples discover the secret of devoting their marriages and their families to the task of serving others, marriages in our nation will be strengthened.

More than playing together, serving together creates a sense of meaning and thankfulness. Playing golf or tennis, hiking, walking, running, gardening, and even dieting together are wonderful experiences, but they are all self-focused. Building a house for a deserving single mom, volunteering as camp counselors, adopting and providing for an aging widow, working together in public service, taking mission trips together, mentoring and coaching together, or counseling as a team are all others-focused.

When a couple invests in others, their focus grows beyond the needs and desires of their marriage. A serendipitous thing happens here: Hidden talents and latent strengths are uncovered. These fresh discoveries feed our appreciation and admiration of each other, and— here's the kicker—intimacy and romance are rekindled.

May your days of service bring you years of happiness!

Love thrives in the face of all life's hazards, save one—neglect.

—John Dryden

He pointed to her and
mouthed the words,
"I love you."

The Tornado's Silver Lining

The honeymoon was a dream, and after the first month of "playing house," Rick and Cindi thought their honeymoon might last forever. Then came the unthinkable.

They heard the warnings on television and radio, urging people to go to the safest rooms of their homes. The sirens blasted that irritating tone that rattles walls.

Cindi had never been through a tornado warning, and she was terrified. Rick had matter-of-factly gathered blankets and pillows, throwing them into the bathtub. Cindi's grip on his arm tightened as they closed the bathroom door. Once Rick had arranged the blankets and pillows, they both climbed into the tub, pulled the blankets over themselves, and with their arms wrapped around each other, waited. By then they could hear the distant roar, which grew louder by the second.

It sounded as if the tornado were cutting a path right through their first-floor apartment. They were smothered by the roar of wind. Then the intensity began to fade, and they experienced an eerie silence.

With the blanket still draped around their shoulders, they opened the bathroom door, expecting the adjoining room to be gone—but nothing had changed. Cindi's Coke glass was still on the kitchen counter. The dirty dishes were still in the sink; even the morning paper was still spread across the table. But when they opened their front door, reality hit hard. The scene from their doorway could have come from the cutting-room floor of *Twister*. They saw empty lots across the street where their neighbors' houses had stood. Vehicles were scattered everywhere; paper, clothes, splintered two-by-fours, and uprooted trees jumbled together as though someone had mixed an odd, giant tossed salad. Then came the sounds—

cries for help, moans, screams, barking dogs, and distant sirens.

Rick noticed that Cindi was no longer sobbing. She had the look of confident determination that a woman gets when she knows exactly what has to be done and how to do it. They both got to work immediately, and their apartment became the center of operations.

Rick helped in the search and rescue, while Cindi comforted the hurting and handed out supplies, including every blanket, pillow, and towel they owned—even the shower gifts they had decided to return. They gave their bed to the family of six down the block. Cindi tirelessly provided food, water, and hot coffee for the workers, while Rick pulled people from the disaster. They were both running on adrenaline.

96

During a short break, Rick returned to the apartment for a drink of water. There he saw his new wife, unaware of his presence, comforting Mrs. Thomas, who had lived in the big two-story house on the corner. Everything Mrs. Thomas owned, even her yappy little poodle, had disappeared. Mrs. Thomas sat in shock over her loss, and Cindi listened attentively to her pain. She cared deeply about the woman and her devastation. Even in the horror of these moments, nothing seemed to daunt Cindi's spirit.

Finally, Rick got her attention—just a glance and a message. He pointed to her and mouthed the words, "I love you."

Shortly after Rick's visit, Cindi caught a glimpse of him helping to pull a half-buried ten-year-old girl from beneath a pile of shattered wall and broken tree limbs. As the youngster hugged Rick, Cindi's eyes flooded with pride. "That's my husband out there," Cindi muttered to no one. "Thank you, God! Thank you for Rick. Keep him safe," she prayed. God was listening.

That night when Rick and Cindi lay on their bare floor to sleep, they were wrapped in each other's arms, not because they were still "playing house," not because they were afraid to let go of each other, and not because they were cold. Rick and Cindi were wrapped in each other's arms because, for them, this was a holy moment. They had found a new level of closeness by doing something for others. As

Rick and Cindi came near to losing everything they had, they discovered a new treasure for their marriage.

Reflections . . .

What special times of ministering to others have you and your spouse shared? How have these experiences enriched your relationship?

_____

_____

_____

_____

_____

_____

_____

_____

_____

_____

_____

_____

CHAPTER SEVEN

Finding Forgiveness

$\mathcal{B}$e subject to one another in the fear of Christ. Above all, love each other deeply, because love covers over a multitude of faults and differences. Forgive the grievances you are holding against each other; let love bind the hurtful wounds. Let My Son's peace rule in your hearts as I continue to build your house.

My Enduring Love and Commitment,

Your God of Restoration

—from Ephesians 5:21; 1 Peter 4:8; Colossians 3:13–16; Psalms 127:1; 138:8

Betrayal may be the most painful emotion to deal with; the pain it brings certainly creates long-lasting hurt. It can come in many shapes: infidelity, deceit, disloyalty, dishonesty. The outcome is the same—undermined trust, emotional torment, and thoughts of retaliation. We have probably all heard people say that they just don't seem able to forgive, as though they had some genetic defect that physically prevents them from forgiving. But in marriage, forgiveness is not an option; it is a necessity.

To forgive means that we choose to give up the right to hurt the one who has hurt us. It is a conscious choice. To make that choice, however, we must be aware of the pain. That's why so many counselors ask clients to journal, to write out the hurt inflected by the offender. Acknowledging and describing these painful memories is the first step in dealing constructively with the hurt. Once the true feelings are out in the open, forgiveness becomes possible.

Granted, it's tough for us to forget past wrongs; only God can do that. But we can pardon the guilt and refuse to keep punishing the offender. When we give up the right to hurt the one who has hurt us, we grant the offender the grace to start over. When powered by forgiveness, unbelievable transformations can occur.

Forgiveness is the most unique concept to come from the Christian faith. When God forgives us, He forgets the guilt and the sin. His forgiveness empowers us to begin again. He doesn't trap us or label us or gripe at us; He removes the failure and encourages us to try again.

When we truly understand God's forgiveness, we will be more eager to forgive others.

The choice is ours.

Marriages that last involve the union of two good forgivers.

—unknown

Everything in her apartment began to remind her of treasured moments with Tom.

The Relationship Resurrection

Tom was clueless and stunned.

They'd had some rocky moments at first, but over the last few years, everything had seemed to settle down. In fact, Tom had recently commented to a friend that he and Rhonda were about to celebrate twenty-five years of marriage and that things had never been better.

"We really understand each other," he'd said.

That's why Rhonda's note was so shocking. Surely it was a terrible joke! It must be a joke. But it was not.

Tom quickly surveyed the house only to discover that all traces of Rhonda had disappeared. Pictures and knickknacks, clothes and personal items, china and silver, even the old rocker she had inherited from her grandmother—Rhonda had taken everything connected to her. He looked at the note again as his shock turned to anger.

"Tom, I'm tired of pretending. Our marriage is dead. Don't try to find me. The divorce papers will be served tomorrow. Just sign them, and let's bury this dead relationship. Rhonda."

Never, not even for one moment, had Tom considered that he and Rhonda had serious problems, much less that they would get divorced. How could he have been so blind? How could she have been so unhappy and not talked to him? The sting of her deception, punctuated by the painful finality of the divorce decree, left Tom drained, distrusting, and cynical.

In spite of the comfort his friends offered him and the devoted support of his two grown children, Tom pulled away, withdrawing from those close to him and losing himself in work.

While Tom wandered the maze of doubt and despair, his friends and family continued to ask God for a miracle—a resurrected marriage.

As the divorce became final and for months afterward, Rhonda began to seriously question her actions. Everything in her apartment began to remind her of treasured moments with Tom. God began peeling the blindness away from her eyes. She had discarded the most treasured part of her life. After all, Tom had in his own way, and sometimes without his knowledge, helped her to become who she was. In fact, he was the one who had encouraged her to try new things. He had instilled in her a confidence that she had turned against him. He was far from perfect, but so was she. Could she get Tom back? Could the love that had died be resurrected?

It took several phone conversations before Tom agreed to meet Rhonda for coffee. Although Rhonda was unassuming and penitent, Tom struggled. He couldn't see beyond his pain, but his pain meant there was still hope.

After several discussions, and with the encouragement of their kids, Tom and Rhonda began attending a marriage-therapy group. At first they felt like misfits—after all, they were divorced—but they soon discovered their issues were the same as the others'. These couples were struggling with power and control, communication and conflict, trust and expectations—just like Tom and Rhonda. With the help of the counselor, they were working on their differences. Tom and Rhonda often found themselves offering warnings against divorce as a solution. After each session Tom and Rhonda talked for hours. As time passed, Tom felt his pain diminishing and being replaced by a willing forgiveness.

Then after an ordinary evening of group shar-
ing and relationship building, Tom announced
he had a question. With five unsuspecting
couples giving him their full attention, he
turned to Rhonda and asked, "Rhonda, will you
honor me by becoming my wife, again?"

Rhonda shouted, "Yes, oh yes!"

The next time the marriage-therapy group
met, a strange thing happened. Instead of
spending their time discussing issues and problems, these new friends joined with Tom and
Rhonda's children in a resurrection ceremony.
Tom and Rhonda were married again, but this
time the vows joined a man and a woman who
were fully aware of the meaning of "for better
or for worse." They had been to both edges of
marriage, and now they could talk about it.

Reflections . . .

How has the power of forgiveness blessed your marriage?

_____
_____
_____
_____
_____
_____
_____
_____
_____
_____
_____
_____
_____
_____
_____

Printed in the United States
By Bookmasters